bead

bead

Designs by
Elizabeth Bower

MURDOCH BOOKS

contents

techniques

projects

Introduction

Beads have been valued since ancient times for their beauty and delicacy. The earliest known examples, made of teeth and bone and designed to be worn as pendants, date back to 38,000 BC. In early times, beads would have been basic in form and fashioned from whatever materials were at hand, but as long ago as the third or fourth century BC, a method of mass-producing glass beads was developed in Southeast Asia. The resulting tiny beads were traded worldwide for 2000 years. Ancient Egypt was another centre for beads, hand-made from stone and later glass.

Throughout the ages, beads have been extensively traded, by nomadic peoples who found them a convenient way of carrying wealth, and by European traders and colonists, who used them to deal with the peoples of other continents. Beads have also been used for religious purposes; indeed, the word bead comes from the old English 'bede', meaning prayer. Rosary beads are perhaps the best-known example of this use. Beads have also had symbolic and superstitious meaning — to ward off evil or attract fertility, or to imply power, friendship or love.

The uses of beads today are primarily ornamental. Whether made from precious or semi-precious gems, shell, glass, ceramic, seeds, wood, stone, bone, plastic or other materials, they are one of the most versatile of all decorative items. They can be strung, wired, glued or sewn to make jewellery or homewares or to decorate clothing. The uses to which they can be put are limited only by your imagination.

This book presents 23 original, contemporary designs, graded roughly in order of difficulty. The tools needed for these projects can be easily found at any jewellery or bead store and at many craft stores. Although not expensive, there are different qualities of tools and therefore different prices; as with all crafts, to achieve the best possible result from your efforts, buy the best tools and materials you can afford.

For the first-time beader, the number and variety of beads and jewellery components in a craft store can be overwhelming. The trick when starting off is to decide on one or two projects and concentrate on getting the materials for those projects only. When you have familiarized yourself with the techniques and components used, you will be able to build on your knowledge and progress to more complicated designs.

Beads and findings

The following are some of the basic components used in making beaded jewellery and other items. In addition to beads of many types, there are various other components (usually metal) that are known as findings.

AB crystal This is a type of crystal with a reflective coating, giving the bead a shiny, rainbow finish. AB stands for Aurora Borealis (the Northern Lights) and the effect is similar. Crystals and beads with an AB finish are available in all sizes from seed beads to large crystals.

Artist's wire This tin-plated copper wire is available in a variety of colours and thicknesses, and used for stringing beads when a flexible but semi-rigid form is called for.

Belcher chain A style of chain that has half-round wire links.

Bell cap A decorative metal dome used to cover the ends of beads.

Bicone A type of diamond-shaped faceted crystal bead; they come in various sizes.

Clasp A component used to secure necklaces and bracelets. There are several types, including parrot clasps, magnetic clasps and screw clasps.

Eye pin A round wire post with a looped circular end (the eye). Beads can be threaded onto the post before being attached to other components.

Florist's tape Green tape used to bind flowers and cover their stems; also used in jewellery making to bind the ends of wires.

AB crystals A special reflective coating gives these beads and crystals an iridescent shimmer.

half beads Flat on one side, these can be glued; some have holes either end and can be sewn.

crystal beads Very precisely cut, these beads add a luxurious sparkle to special items.

glass beads A wide variety of shapes, sizes and finishes is available.

pearl beads Whether natural or artificial (glass or plastic), pearls have a lovely lustre.

seed beads These small beads are formed from a glass tube cut into smaller sections.

Head pin A round wire post with a flattened end (the head). Beads can be threaded onto the post before the end of the post is formed into an eyelet, then attached to other components.

Jump rings Wire rings that are used to link components. Open jump rings have a split allowing them to be opened so that they can be attached directly to other components. Closed jump rings have been soldered into a circle. Jump rings are available in various sizes. Depending on the size and weight of the beads used, you will need to use different thicknesses and sizes of jump ring.

Memory wire Coiled steel wire that retains its circular shape. It is available in various ring, bangle and choker diameters and can be cut to give as few or as many continuous loops as you require.

Parrot clasp Teardrop-shaped clasp with a spring opening mechanism, used for fastening necklaces and bracelets. These are available in a variety of sizes and finishes.

Pony beads This is the name given to larger seed beads.

Seed bead Tiny glass beads available in a wide variety of colours and finishes. They are made from glass rods cut into small sections.

Spacer bar A flat, elongated oval or rectangular shape with holes, used to connect multiple strands together on chokers or bracelets.

Tiger tail A type of nylon-coated metal thread onto which beads can be strung; it is a very strong and flexible material.

belcher chain A chain with circular, half-round links.

head pins Used when beads are to be attached at one end only.

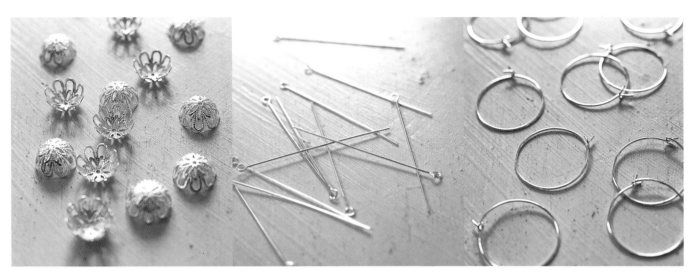

bell caps Decorative metal findings used to hold beads in place.

eye pins The eye at the end allows a bead to be linked on both sides.

findings Metal components such as these earring hoops are known as findings.

jump rings Small round rings, either open or closed, used for linking components together.

parrot clasp Metal clasp with an opening mechanism like a parrot's beak.

spacer bars Used to separate multiple strands in bracelets or chokers.

Basic tools

Below is a list of basic tools you will need when making the designs from this book. Some projects may require more specific tools. These tools can be found at jewellery suppliers, craft stores and some hardware stores.

Round-nose pliers These have two round, tapering jaws around which the posts of head and eye pins can be twisted to give eyelets of varying diameters. They should not be serrated; this applies to all types of pliers for beading work. The tapered ends allow you to hold and work with very fine components.

Snipe-nose or chain-nose pliers These are useful for gripping components while working with them. In many cases you will use a pair of pliers in each hand to open and close components such as jump rings or to attach one component to another.

Flat-nose pliers The blunt, squared-off ends of these pliers make them useful for holding components steady, but they cannot be used to bend wire into eyelets. They can, however, be used to straighten wire or eye or head posts.

Side cutters Similar in appearance to pliers but with two metal blades to cut head pins, eye pins and chains.

Ruler The metal type is preferable to plastic, as it is more durable.

Tape measure For measuring items that are longer than the ruler, or that are curved. The fibreglass type is preferable to plastic, as it is less likely to stretch and distort.

Scissors Keep separate pairs, one for paper and one for fabric; using scissors on paper blunts them, so that they will not then cut fabric easily.

Safety glasses These should be worn when cutting metal findings with side cutters so that the cut-off pieces do not fly into your eyes and cause injury.

Design fundamentals

Proportions are crucial in jewellery making, so it's important to plan your designs in their initial stages to avoid making mistakes and wasting money. When making wearable items, the following factors need to be considered.

Weight

Consider the weight of your beads when constructing your designs. Don't choose beads that are too heavy to be supported by the structure of the item or that will be uncomfortable to wear. Avoid placing beads with sharp edges on chokers and other pieces that are worn close on the body, as they will be uncomfortable.

Form

Use shapes that complement each other. If you are using organic round and oval beads, a square one will look out of place. Select the right bead for the form you are making; for example, using elongated beads on a choker will prevent the piece from sitting naturally, as it will develop kinks around the beads.

Proportions

A common mistake in beading is choosing components that don't fit together. Beads, thread, end pins and head pins are available in a variety of sizes. Make sure you select corresponding thicknesses so that the thread or post you are using will pass through the hole of your smallest bead.

Basic techniques

These techniques are employed throughout the book and, once perfected, can be adapted to a wide variety of uses.

Opening and closing jump rings

This technique is used to add beads and other components to the jump rings, or to connect a series of jump rings to form a chain to which other components are then attached.

1 Hold the jump ring on either side of its split using either snipe-nose or flat-nose pliers. Swing the jump ring open by pulling one side of the ring toward you and pushing the other side away, as shown in the photograph below.

2 To close the ring, repeat the process in the opposite direction.

3 To close a gap in a jump ring, hold either side with pliers and gently move the sides back and forth while slowly pushing them together. This technique avoids distortion of the rings and allows you to close the ring securely.

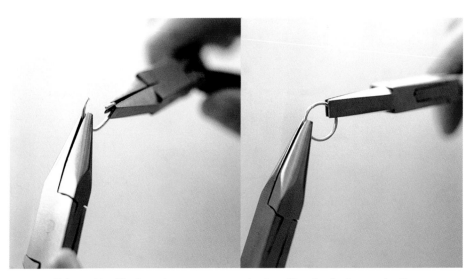

step one Pull one side of the jump ring towards you and push the other side away.

step two Close the ring by reversing the process in Step 1.

Looping head pins and eye pins

1 Thread one or more beads onto a head or eye pin, leaving at least 1 cm (⅜ in) of post exposed.

2 Cut the post to approximately 1 cm (⅜ in) using side cutters. Wear safety glasses when doing this as the metal offcuts may fly off and cause damage to your eyes.

3 Hold the remaining end of the post with the top of the round-nose pliers. Bend the wire around the pliers to create a circular loop or eyelet. You may need to bend the wire in two movements.

4 To straighten the loop, so it sits directly on top of the post, position the round-nose pliers inside the loop. Rest the tip of the pliers against the base of the loop (near the post) on the closed side. Gently push down towards the post so the loop rolls into position and rests on top of the post, as shown in the photograph.

5 If you are looping the end of an eye pin, make sure you create the second loop in the opposite direction to the first, thus creating an 'S' shape. Straighten both loops so they sit flat in the same direction.

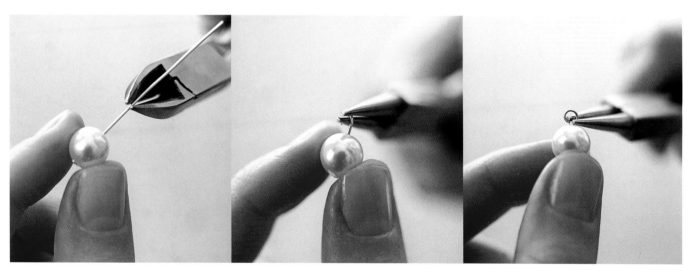

step two Cut the post, leaving approximately 1 cm (⅜ in) exposed.

step three Roll the end of the post around a pair of round-nose pliers.

step four Gently push the pliers down towards the post.

Wrapping head pin posts

This technique is a more secure method of linking or attaching beads. It's best to use this technique if you are using heavy beads or fine wires, so the links will not open over time.

1 Thread a bead onto a head pin or eye pin. Make sure the post has approximately 3 cm (1¼ in) of excess wire.

2 Bend the end of the head pin around the round-nose pliers at the appropriate position, depending on the size of the loop you require; that is, use the base of the pliers to create a large loop or the tip for a smaller loop. Wrap the post 360 degrees around the pliers.

3 Open the loop with the snipe-nose pliers and thread onto the piece of jewellery or add the component to which you are linking the bead.

4 Close and hold the loop, by clamping with the round-nose pliers.

5 Hold the end of the wire with the snipe-nose pliers and wrap it 360 degrees around the post at the top of the bead in a full circle.

6 Cut off the excess wire with the side cutters.

step one Thread a bead onto a pin.

step two Bend the end of the post around the round-nose pliers.

step five Wrap the end of the wire around the post at the top of the bead.

step six Cut off the excess wire with the side cutters.

Linking head pins and eye pins

This technique is used to link beaded head pins or eye pins to other components in the design.

1 Once the pin has been beaded and an eyelet made in the end, open the end post with snipe-nose pliers.

2 Swing the loop open like a door (as for opening jump rings, page 16) so the circular shape is not distorted.

3 Attach or link to the chain or component then swing the loop closed, making sure each loop is tightly secured and there are no gaps.

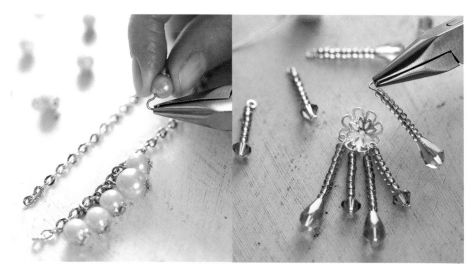

step two With snipe-nose pliers, open the eyelet at the end of the head pin.

step three Here, several beaded head pins are being attached to a bell cap.

Making clasps and earring hooks

There are many commercial clasps and earring hooks available, but you may choose to create your own as a cost-effective measure or to retain the handmade quality of your work. You can recycle excess wire that has been cut off head pins or eye pins.

Use 0.8—0.9 mm (19–20 gauge) wire. Cut the wire into a 3 cm (1¼ in) length for a clasp or 5 cm (2 in) for earring hooks.

1 To make earring hooks, create a small eyelet by looping one end of the wire into an eyelet using the tip of your round-nose pliers (see Basic techniques, page 17).

2 Position the base of the pliers approximately 1 cm (⅜ in) above the eyelet. Make sure the eyelet is facing away from the pliers. Using your fingers, push both sides of the wire around the pliers so they meet, creating a large teardrop-shaped loop.

3 Using the tip of the round-nose pliers, slightly bend the end of the post.

4 To smooth the cut ends of the hook, rub with 1000-grade emery paper, which can be bought at a hardware store.

5 You can also make clasps for bracelets and necklaces in a similar fashion; use the technique above but form the wire into an S shape in which one loop is

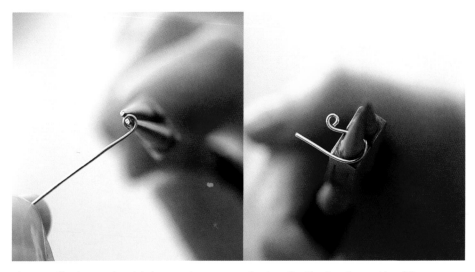

step one Create a small eyelet at one end of the wire using round-nose pliers.

step two Position the pliers and bend the wire around them.

larger than the other. You will need to leave an opening at the end of this larger loop; this gap should be big enough for the loop or jump ring to which it is to be joined to pass through it, but not so big to allow the necklace or bracelet to come loose and fall off. Close the small eyelet at the other end of the clasp completely (when later attaching it to an item of jewellery, you will need to reopen and reclose it as explained on page 19).

6 Smooth the cut ends of the clasp as explained in Step 4.

This type of clasp is useful when making jewellery for someone who finds parrot clasps too small and fiddly to manage, or to match the scale of jewellery items that use large components.

Hints

Use a fishing tackle box or ice-cube tray to organize and store your beads and findings.

Removable putty, such as Blu-Tac, is great for securing beads on half-finished projects; for example, attach a blob to the end of memory wire, tiger tail, or nylon thread to stop beads falling off while you work.

To stop beads rolling around while you're working, use a shallow tray, and cover the base with a piece of felt. Beading suppliers also stock inexpensive ready-made plastic trays. These have several compartments for storing beads as you work, as well as grooves in standard bracelet and necklace lengths, into which you can place beads and rearrange them until you have made a pleasing design.

When working with ribbons, cords or other materials that might fray, coat the cut ends with a small amount of clear nail polish.

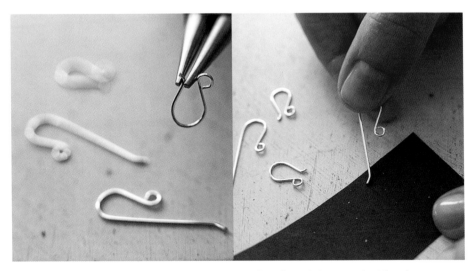

step three Slightly bend the end of the wire hook.

step four Smooth the cut ends of the wire using emery paper.

Pearl choker

Pearls have a soft, rich sheen that adds a

luxurious glow to any skin tone. This stylish

choker, constructed with imitation pearl beads

on silk satin cord, gives a more casual cast

to the traditional pearl necklace.

The same simple technique would lend itself well

to other interpretations, such as leather thonging

with wooden or ceramic beads or thin cord with

crystal beads. Remember to check that your

chosen cord is thin enough to pass through the

hole in your smallest bead.

Materials
24 plastic pearl beads, 14 mm (9/16 in) diameter
  (or number required to fit neck size)
1.5 m (60 in) round silk cord
Clear nail varnish

Tools
Round-nose pliers
Scissors

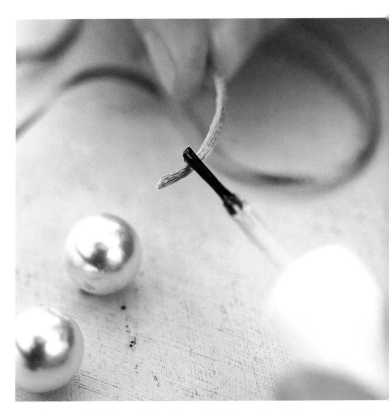

step one Paint the end of the silk cord with clear nail varnish to prevent fraying.

1 Tie a tight knot in one end of the length of silk cord. Neaten the end by cutting off the excess cord, leaving approximately 5 mm (¼ in). Dab a small amount of clear nail varnish on the end to prevent the cord from fraying. Cut the other end of the silk cord on an angle and coat the last 2.5 mm (⅛ in) of it in clear nail varnish to preserve the point (as shown in the photograph above).

2 Prepare the pearl beads by enlarging the hole in each one using small round-nose pliers. To do this, thread a bead onto the tapered shank of the pliers and push down firmly towards the handle, at the same time twisting the bead back and forth. You should notice the opening of the bead flaring out. Repeat for the other end of the hole. Enlarge the holes in all of the beads in this way, to make it easier to thread them onto the silk cord.

3 When the clear nail polish on the end of the cord is dry and firm, thread the first bead onto the cord so it is resting on the knot. Once it is in place, tie another knot in the cord to hold the pearl in place. Make sure the knot sits close to the bead: to do this, make a large, loose slip knot and, as you slowly pull the knot closed, roll it back down the cord towards the bead with fingers.

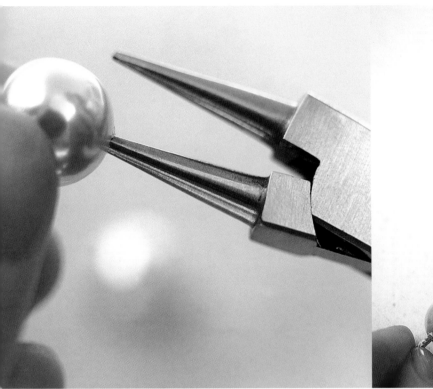

two Enlarge the holes in the beads using a pair of round-nose pliers.

step four Knot the cord between each pearl bead.

4 Leave a 25 cm (10 in) length of silk cord and tie another knot. This is where you will begin to add the beads for the choker proper. Thread on another pearl bead (see the photograph illustrating this step above) and make a knot after it. Add another pearl bead next to this knot, then make another knot. Repeat until you have strung and knotted about 22 pearls. You may alter the number of pearls to fit your neck size.

5 Leave a 30 cm (12 in) length of cord, make another knot and finish with a pearl bead knotted in place. Cut the excess cord with scissors, leaving 5 mm (¼ in), and coat the end in nail varnish.

Variations

Tie the choker around your neck, fastening it with a bow. A choker is meant to be worn quite high on the neck, but you can make a longer necklace that can be worn wrapped as a choker or a bracelet as well as a necklace. Leave bigger gaps between the pearl beads and allow extra cord if necessary. Using smaller pearl beads will allow fluid movement in the piece and more flexibility when you wear it.

Cushion

A purchased silk cushion cover is embellished with a graduated sprinkling of half-pearls to create an inexpensive and striking designer pillow. The pearls are simply glued on using an adhesive that is designed to bond rhinestones and sequins to fabric, and which dries clear and washable. Glues of this type are available at beading, craft and haberdashery suppliers.

Materials

1 beige silk dupion cushion cover, 45 cm (18 in) square

1 cushion insert, 45 cm (18 in) square

Clear-drying, washable fabric glue such as Gem-Tac (available from craft and beading suppliers)

45 plastic half-pearls, 16 mm ($5/8$ in) diameter

55 plastic half-pearls, 12 mm ($1/2$ in) diameter

90 plastic half-pearls, 10 mm ($7/16$ in) diameter

20 plastic half pearls, 8 mm ($5/16$ in) diameter

step two Glue large and medium beads in a random pattern.

step three Glue medium and smaller beads slightly further apart.

1 Wash, dry and iron the cushion cover, to make sure that the fabric is clean so that the glue will adhere properly.

2 Lay the cushion cover on a clean, flat surface. Start gluing all of the 16 mm (⅝ in) pearls and two-thirds of the 12 mm (½ in) pearls across the entire width of the cushion, filling the lower 8–10 cm (3¼–4 in) of the fabric. To do this, randomly place small dots of glue on the fabric at 20 mm (¾ in) intervals and gently place a pearl on top of each. Work from left to right (or the opposite direction if you are left handed), placing five dots of glue at a time then covering them with the pearls. The pearls should be sitting closely together but not touching. Be careful not to make the glue dots too big, as the excess will ooze out, leaving visible rings around the pearls.

3 Glue the remaining 12 mm (½ in) pearls, all of the 10 mm (⁷⁄₁₆ in) pearls and two-thirds of the 8 mm (⁵⁄₁₆ in) pearls across the width of the cushion, covering the next 20 cm (8 in) of the fabric. Place dots of glue 30–40 mm (1¼–1½ in) apart to create a graduated scattering.

4 Glue the remaining 8 mm (⁵⁄₁₆ in) pearls across the last 17 cm (6½ in) of the cushion, placing them 50–60 mm (2–2½ in) apart.

option Stitch seed beads down in groups of three.

option Use beads to highlight fabric designs or stitching.

Options

Make a matching lampshade with the same effect, by following the steps above, dividing the shade into four zones from bottom (most encrusted) to top (least encrusted). Use a lampshade made of opaque fabric so that the pearls don't create strange shadows when the light is switched on.

Make other gorgeous cushion covers using luxurious striped or floral fabric and embellishing over the pattern with beads, as shown in the photographs above. To stitch seed beads onto fabric, simply double-thread a needle, knot the ends together then insert it into the fabric from back to front to emerge at the desired point on the design. Place three beads onto the needle. Lay the beads in position on the fabric and pass the needle back through the fabric, underneath and back up through the initial entry point, thus creating a circle of thread. Bring the needle back through the three beads to secure. Add another three beads and repeat the process until the design is covered sufficiently.

Stitch larger beads on separately, ensuring each one sits nicely on the fabric before passing the needle through again.

Hint

To stitch individual beads onto fabric, use a double-threaded needle and secure them as follows: bring the needle to the front of the fabric, thread on a bead and pass the needle through to the back of the fabric. Bring the needle up again through the first hole, then take it down through the second hole without stitching through the bead. As you pull the thread through, ensure that one of the threads goes on either side of the bead.

Chandelier

The glittering of light on cut glass brings a room to life. Even in daylight, sunbeams will play on the crystals suspended from this simple chandelier. At night, the electric light globe will make the clear glass droplets sparkle.

Chandelier crystals are available at craft stores and bead suppliers; vintage chandelier crystals may often be found at garage sales and antique markets. Lampshade frames can be bought at craft, haberdashery and lighting suppliers.

Materials

1 can silver spray paint
1 round lampshade frame
260 two-holed chandelier crystals,
    12 mm (½ in) in diameter
8 frilly drop chandelier crystals, 50 mm
    (2 in) long
392 silver jump rings, 10 mm (⅜ in) diameter
Fine wire

Tools

Snipe-nose pliers
Flat-nose pliers
Saw frame or fret saw (optional; available
    from hardware stores)
Flat file (optional)
Newspaper

step one If necessary, saw off unwanted parts of the lampshade frame.

step three Link two-holed crystals together with jump rings.

1 If you are unable to buy a simple round lampshade frame, buy a standard cylindrical frame and saw off the additional posts. To do this, put the frame on a flat surface with the end you want to cut off protruding over the edge of the work surface. Cut off each leg of the frame, using an up-and-down motion and keeping the blade of the saw horizontal. File the edges, if necessary, to remove burrs.

2 Lay down some newspaper in a well-ventilated area and spray the frame with silver spray paint. Leave to dry thoroughly while you proceed with the construction of the chandelier drops.

3 To create the crystal drops, link the two-holed crystals together using jump rings. Open the jump rings (see basic instructions, page 16) using the snipe-nose and flat-nose pliers, attach a crystal and close. Repeat the process to create 24 strands each containing 15 linked crystals.

4 Using jump rings (as above), link a frilly crystal drop to eight of the 24 strands.

5 When the lampshade frame is dry, begin to attach the crystal strands to the large circular rim of the frame. Place six strands in each quarter of the shade, with every third strand having a frilly crystal drop.

four Add a frilly drop to eight of the crystal strands.

step six Attach the crystal strands to the lampshade frame.

Make sure the crystal pendants face outwards when attached.

6 Hang the chandelier on a pendant light: first, remove the light bulb and unscrew the plastic cylinder surrounding the fitting. Slide the lampshade frame on top of the fitting, screw it into place with the plastic cylinder and replace the bulb. When the chandelier is hanging in position, adjust the crystal links so they sit evenly around the frame and the frame balances evenly.

7 Secure the jump rings in position on the frame with small ties of fine wire, twisted in place using a pair of snipe-nose pliers.

Variations

You can adapt this design for a standard lampshade by using a cylindrical standard lampshade frame. Follow steps two to five above, making sure the crystal strands are the same length as the frame. Link the crystal strands to the top of the frame and again at the bottom, allowing the frilly drops to hang below the frame.

Alternatively, attach the crystal strands to the bottom edge of a plain fabric or paper lampshade. The fabric or paper covering can be pierced with an awl to accept the jump rings and will hold them in position.

Memory wire ring

Memory wire is formed in a continuous spiral and can be cut to give as many coils as are needed. It retains its shape while also having enough flexibility to fit almost any size of finger.

In this exuberant design, seed beads cover the coils of wire, while a variety of feature beads give colour and sparkle.

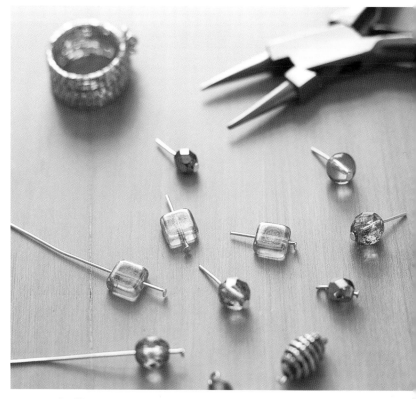

step five Place each bead onto a head pin and cut off excess wire.

Materials

1 packet ring memory wire

14 head pins, 14 mm (⅝ in) long

6 jump rings, 14 mm (⅝ in) round

10 g (⅓ oz) seed beads

14 feature beads, 5–7 mm (¼ in) long, in assorted shapes and colours

Tools

Round-nose pliers

Snipe-nose pliers

Flat-nose pliers

Side cutters

Safety glasses

1 Cut the memory wire with the side cutters, allowing for 6 coils. Curl the end of the ring wire (using round-nose pliers) to make a 3 mm (⅛ in) loop that sits on top of the ring. Straighten if needed with the snipe-nose pliers.

2 Thread seed beads onto the ring, filling all six coils. Make sure the beads end level with the same point at which you began.

3 Cut excess wire with side cutters, leaving enough to make a 3 mm (⅛ in) loop (as in Step 1). Round and loop the remaining wire with round-nose pliers, securing all of the seed beads onto the memory wire.

4 Connect the jump rings together (see basic instructions, page 16) using the snipe- and flat-nose pliers. Attach the jump rings to either side of the looped memory wire, so they rest along the top of the ring.

5 Place each bead onto a head pin and cut excess wire with side cutters, leaving about 7 mm (¼ in). Curl the end of each pin into an eyelet (see Basic techniques, page 17).

6 Attach the beaded end posts along the jump rings so the beads are distributed to give a good mix of shapes and colours. There should be some movement so the beads move around when the ring is worn.

Drink identifiers

Adorn the stem of elegant glassware with jewellery that serves the double purpose of decorating the glass and identifying it. This recent party phenomenon removes the problem of remembering exactly where you put your glass and whether it is the half-full one or the almost-empty one beside it.

A selection of pretty beads in colour groups is one solution — use a different colour for each guest — and the metal findings are simply small earring hoops, available from bead and craft suppliers.

Materials

3 pairs silver drop earrings with threadable
   hoops, 25 mm (1 in) diameter
18 jump rings, 4 mm (⅛ in) diameter
54 silver head pins, 30 mm (1¼ in) long
For each of the six colour schemes (pink,
   purple, silver, cream, brown and gold), you
   will need nine beads: 8 round beads, 5 mm
   (³⁄₁₆ in) diameter, and 1 oval bead, 15 mm
   (⅝ in) long (to make a total of 54 beads)

Tools

Round-nose pliers
Snipe-nose pliers
Flat-nose pliers
Side cutters
Safety glasses

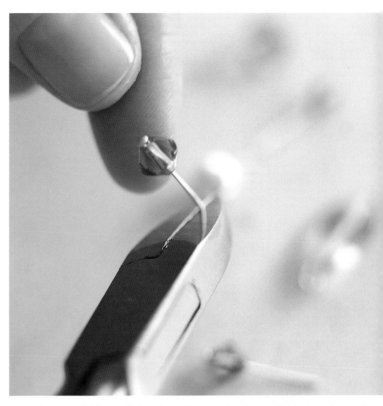

step one Cut the post of each head pin, leaving 10 mm (⅜ in) above the bead.

1 Place each of the beads on a head pin. Cut the post of each head pin using the side cutters, leaving 10 mm (⅜ in) of post above the bead, as shown in the photograph above. Create an eyelet on the exposed end of each pin by curling the post around the shaft of the round-nose pliers (for further instructions on how to do this, see Basic techniques, page 17).

2 Using the snipe-nose and flat-nose pliers, link three jump rings together into one chain section (see Basic techniques, page 16, for further details). Repeat this process with the remaining jump rings to make a total of six chain sections.

3 Attach each group of jump rings to a hoop. To do this, open the hoop and slide the jump ring at one end of each section over the hoop, as shown in the photograph. Close the hoop again to ensure the rings don't fall off.

4 Connect the beads to the jump ring chain sections. First attach a 15 mm (⅝ in) oval bead on its pin to the end jump ring, using the snipe-nose pliers (for further instructions on how to do this, see Basic techniques, page 19). Using the same method, attach one 5 mm (³⁄₁₆ inch) bead by its pin to the end jump ring, on either side of the oval bead.

three Attach each group of three jump rings to a hoop.

step five Attach pairs of beads to each jump ring, one on each side.

5 To the next jump ring in the chain, attach one 5 mm (³⁄₁₆ inch) bead on each side of the ring. Lastly, attach the remaining two beads on either side of the top jump ring (the one that is connected to the hoop.)

6 Undo the hoop to attach it around the stem of a glass. Make sure you remove the drink identifiers before washing the glasses, and be careful to hook the hoop closed when the marker is not in use, so the beads do not slip off the hoop.

Hints

Sets of drink identifiers make great gifts, as they're so easy to construct. You can vary the colour schemes and the types of beads to make themed or seasonal attachments.

Use this technique to make keyrings or handbag charms by adding different connections. Follow the steps above and attach a keyring finding instead of an earring hoop.

Chandelier earrings

These spectacular earrings will glitter and glow like chandeliers as you move. To create them, choose drop earring hoops with an open end so that beads and other jewellery findings can be easily threaded onto the hoop itself.

Materials
1 pair gold threadable hoops
2 gold brass stampings, 20 mm (¾ in) long
  (these can be found at bead stores)
1 pair gold earring hooks
20 gold head pins, 30 mm (1¼ in) long
40 cm (16 in) gold oval chain
2 gold jump rings, 4 mm (⅛ in) diameter
6 gold opaque crystal beads, 6 mm
  (¼ in) diameter
6 champagne bicone beads, 5 mm
  (³⁄₁₆ in) diameter
36 round glass beads, 4 mm (⅛ in) diameter

Tools
Round-nose pliers
Snipe-nose pliers
Side cutters
Safety glasses

Earring components, clockwise from bottom left: head pins; threadable earring hoops; earring hooks; 2 lengths oval chain; gold brass stamping

steps one and two Thread beads onto head pins, then cut and curl the posts.

Hint

If you cannot find a brass stamping, select an oval 10 mm (⅜ in) bead. Thread it onto an eye pin, then cut the remaining wire with side cutters, leaving 10 mm (⅜ in). Loop the end of the pin using round-nose pliers (see Basic techniques, page 17). One loop should be larger than the other. Attach the smaller loop to the hoop, as in Step 6. Open the larger loop with the snipe-nose pliers, thread on the five beaded head pins and close the loop again.

1 Thread a selection of beads onto the head pins as follows:
- Onto each of eight head pins, thread one round glass bead.
- Onto each of four head pins, thread one bicone bead.
- Onto each of four head pins, thread one opaque gold bead.
- Onto each of two head pins, thread one round glass bead and one bicone bead.
- Onto each of two head pins, thread one round glass bead and one opaque gold bead.

Using side cutters, cut the excess length off the posts, leaving 10 mm (⅜ in) protruding beyond the beads.

2 Using round-nose pliers, curl the post of each head pin to form an eyelet (see Basic techniques, page 17).

3 Using side cutters, cut the chain into two 80 mm (3⅛ in) and two 110 mm (4⅜ in) lengths.

4 Pull the threadable earring hoop open (one end of the loop is not secure, and can be pulled open) and thread the hoop through the last link in a 110 mm (4⅜ in) chain. Thread a 4 mm (⅛ in) round bead onto the hoop, then the last link of the 80 mm (3⅛ in) chain, as shown in the photograph above.

steps four and five Thread beads and chain onto the hoop in the order pictured.

step six Attach beaded head pins to the stamping and assemble the earrings.

5 Continue threading the hoop in sequence as follows: three round beads; one round bead on head pin; one round bead; one gold opaque crystal on head pin; one round bead; round bead and bicone bead on head pin; one round bead; one gold opaque crystal on head pin; one round bead; one round bead on head pin; three round beads; other end of the 80 mm (3⅛ in) chain; one round bead; the other end of the 110 mm (4⅜ in) chain. Refer also to the photographs for the order of components. Finish each earring by reclosing the threadable hoop.

6 Attach the remaining beaded head pins to the bottom edges of the brass stampings, referring to the photographs for the order of the pins. Attach the top of the stamping to the underside of the top of the hoop using a jump ring (see Basic techniques, page 16).

7 Using snipe-nose pliers, attach an earring hook to the top of each hoop.

Charm bracelet

A creative version of the traditional charm

bracelet, this jewelled wristlet employs a variety

of beads to catch the eye. Glass beads in

translucent colours approximate the beauty

of semi-precious gems such as amethysts,

garnets, rubies and diamonds.

Mix beads of different size, shape and colours in

a random pattern of repetition to ensure that you

capture the eclectic look of a charm bracelet.

Materials
Approximately 15 cm (6 in) chain: the length
   may differ depending on your wrist size.
   To check the size, measure your wrist with
   a tape measure so the tape sits firmly
   around the wrist
Beads of various shapes and sizes: the
   number will depend on length of the chain
   — allow one bead per chain link, except for
   the two end links, plus one bead for the
   jump ring extension chain
Head pins, 40 mm (1½ in) long: one per bead
8 jump rings, 5 mm (⅜ in) diameter
1 parrot clasp

Tools
Round-nose pliers
Snipe-nose pliers
Flat-nose pliers
Side cutters
Safety glasses

step two Thread each bead onto a head pin and make a loop at the end of the p[e]

Hints

The wrist is very flexible, so select a medium-weight chain that is not too flimsy and with links large enough to thread the end posts through.

Stick to a simple colour scheme and gather six to eight different styles of bead, repeating each style and colour a few times throughout the bracelet. Choose beads of a similar size and weight to give a bracelet that is balanced in colour and style, and to avoid having one end heavier than the other.

1 Arrange your selection of beads on a tray (see Hints, page 21) in a row, paying attention to the balance and proportion of the arrangement.

2 Thread each bead onto a head pin and trim all but 10 mm (⅜ in) off the post using side cutters. Use round-nose pliers to make a loop, as shown in the photograph above.

3 Attach the beaded head pins one at a time to the chain in the desired order (see Basic techniques, page 19), leaving one link at either end to attach your clasp and jump rings. Add one beaded head pin to each link of the chain until the chain is full.

three Attach one bead to each link of the chain.

step four Make a chain of jump rings and attach the remaining bead to the end.

4 Create the extension, which allows the bracelet to be worn at different lengths. Open the jump rings (see Basic techniques, page 16) and link seven of them together in a chain. Attach the end ring to the last link of chain in the bracelet. At the other end of the jump-ring chain, attach the remaining beaded head pin (in the same manner as for the bracelet). Attention to small details like this adds to the quality of your design.

5 Attach the parrot clasp to the empty link at the other end of the bracelet, using the remaining jump ring. Fasten the clasp to the jump ring that gives the desired size.

Hints

To make a matching necklace, extend the length of the chain (and the corresponding number of beads) to approximately 42 cm (16½ in).

For a finer look, attach beads on every second chain link.

You could also revamp an old evening bag by replacing the chain strap with a handle made using this technique. Add a clasp at each end of the handle to make it detachable.

Table runner

Repetition of a simple flower design unifies this piece, while the different finishes of the beads used — some opaque, some pearlescent, others mirrored — add variety and interest.

When laying out the beads, concentrate them around the edges and at the ends of the runner, so that they will not be in the way of items that you put on top of the runner.

step two Glue the beads down one at a time.

Materials
1 fabric table runner; this can be hand made to match the proportions of an existing table, or bought at a homeware or craft store

Approximately 150 half-round, half-oval, and/or half-teardrop shaped plastic stones or pearls in various colours and finishes, sized from 8 mm (⁵⁄₁₆ in) to 15 mm (⁵⁄₈ in)

Tools
Clear-drying, washable fabric glue such as Gem-Tac (available from craft and beading suppliers)

Large table, to lay out the design

1 Follow any preparation instructions given on the glue; you may have to wash the fabric to avoid pilling. Iron the table runner and lay it on a large flat surface.

2 Lay out the beads and begin to arrange them in a pattern.

3 Once you have achieved a pleasing pattern, lift each bead individually and glue into position, as shown in the photograph above. Make sure not to use too much glue.

4 Allow to dry for 24 hours before use to make sure the glue is secure.

Hints

Use the same technique to make matching napkins. Glue a beaded flower on the corner of each napkin in similar colours.

This technique could also be used to embellish a singlet top, T-shirt or other garment.

Beaded tassel

Wear these beaded tassels as jewellery, as

a pendant or earrings; dress up your home

by using them on soft furnishings; or attach one

to a keyring or handbag and carry it with you.

Once you have mastered the basic tassel-

making process, you will be able to experiment

with variations of size, shape and materials to

create your own unique tassels.

Materials (per drop)
Silver bell cap (with 8 sections)
5 head pins, 40 mm (1⅝ in)
68 pink seed beads
1 pearl, 10 mm (⅜ in)
5 bicone crystal beads, 6 mm (¼ in)
4 teardrop crystals, 10 mm (⅜ in)

Tools
Round-nose pliers
Snipe-nose pliers
Side cutters
Safety glasses
Needle

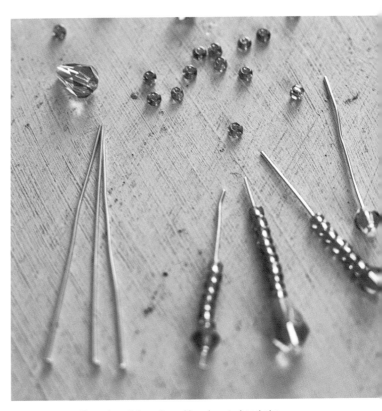

step one Thread crystals and seed beads onto head pins.

1 Thread four of the 6 mm (¼ in) bicone crystals onto head pins and top with seven seed beads to each pin. Thread all of the 10 mm (⅜ in) teardrop crystals onto head pins and top with ten seed beads to each pin. Refer to the photograph above.

2 Using side cutters, cut the excess post from the head pins, leaving a 6 mm (¼ in) length of the metal post protruding. Create an eyelet by turning the exposed metal post around a pair of round-nose pliers (see Basic techniques, page 17).

3 Attach the beaded head pins around the sections of the bell cap, alternating between the bicone crystal pins and the teardrop crystal pins. See the photograph above for details.

4 Thread the pearl onto a head pin and pass the pin through the top of the bell cap, then thread the remaining bicone crystal bead on top of the bell cap. Cut the head pin using side cutters, leaving 10 mm (⅜ in) of post protruding, then create an eyelet as described in Step 2.

5 Use the eyelet at the top of the tassel to attach it to a further fastening, such as an earring hook or a keyring, or to stitch it to ribbon or fabric as a decorative finish.

three Alternate pins around the sections of the bell cap.

step four Pass a head pin through the pearl and the bell cap, then add a bead.

Variations

The basic tassel can be used for a variety of purposes:

• To decorate the end of window-blind cords.

• Attach to a chain and wear as a pendant.

• Attach an earring hook to create earrings.

• Attach to silk cord and use as curtain ties.

• Attach to clip-on earrings and use as weights on a tablecloth.

Jewelled gift-wrapping

A beautifully wrapped present to celebrate a special occasion or festive season, or simply to express love and gratitude, is always welcome. In this case, the wrapping becomes part of the gift, with silken cord and pretty jewels that can be put to use after the present is opened.

Materials

Belcher chain with 3 mm (⅛ in) links

60 silver head pins, 30 mm (1³⁄₁₆ in) long

4 silver coiled end caps

4 m (13 ft) silk cord (rat's tail)

40 pearls, in various sizes from 6–12 mm
   (¼–½ in) diameter

16 bicone crystals, 6 mm (¼ in) diameter

4 oval glass beads, 17 mm (⅝ in) long

Tools

Round-nose pliers

Snipe-nose pliers

Flat-nose pliers

Side cutters

Clear nail varnish

step one Thread individual beads and pearls onto head pins.

step three Attach the beads to the lengths of chain using jump rings.

Hints

This technique can be used to make a lariat necklace, which wraps once or several times around the neck depending on the length of the cord. A lariat necklace is fastened by slipping one weighted (jewelled) end of the cord or chain through a loop at the other.

Turn this design into a pair of earrings by following Steps 2–4 and adding earring hooks to the end of the jump rings.

1 Thread individual beads and pearls onto head pins and cut off the excess metal post with side cutters, leaving 10 mm (⅜ in) of post. Create eyelets in the end of the posts (see Basic techniques, page 17) with round-nose pliers.

2 Cut the belcher chain into four lengths of about 15 links (about 25 mm/1 in).

3 Divide the beads equally into four groups and attach the head pins to the chain links (see Basic techniques, page 19) so that the beads graduate along the lengths of chain, with the larger beads at one end and the smaller at the other (see photograph).

four Coat one end of each length of silk cord with clear nail varnsh.

step five Clamp the end caps on the hardened end of the silk cord.

4 Cut the silk cord into two lengths and coat 10 mm (⅜ in) at one end of each length with clear nail polish to prevent the cord unravelling as you work with it.

5 Once the nail varnish is dry on the ends of the cord, slide the open end of a coiled end cap over the hardened section of cord. Secure the cap onto the cord by clamping the last coil of wire in the end cap between the jaws of the snipe-nose pliers.

6 Wrap the cord around the gift and cut the raw ends so it sits or hangs nicely. Repeat Steps 4 and 5 with the remaining ends of the cord and the remaining end caps.

7 Attach each section of beaded chain to a coiled end cap using snipe-nose pliers.

Chain necklace

This beautiful necklace features multiple pendants of beads on graduated chain lengths suspended from a chain choker. The symmetry of its structure and the triple-bead clusters at the end of each chain create a simple yet opulent effect.

The pictured example uses a type of blackened silver chain and findings, but you could use other finishes if desired.

Materials

Blackened parrot clasp
8 blackened jump rings, 4 mm (³⁄₁₆ in)
2 m (80 in) blackened chain with 5 mm (³⁄₁₆ in) oval links (with unsoldered links)
40 blackened head pins, 30 mm (1⅛ in) long
27 purple-grey round beads, 8 mm (⁵⁄₁₆ in) diameter
3 purple oval beads, 16 mm (⅝ in) long
10 purple flat oval beads, 11 mm (⁷⁄₁₆ in) long

Tools

Round-nose pliers
Snipe-nose pliers
Side cutters
Safety glasses

step one Thread beads onto head pins then make eyelets in the ends of the posts.

step two Cut the chain into graduated lengths.

1 Thread the individual beads onto head pins, cutting off all but 10 mm (⅜ in) of the exposed post with side cutters. Make an eyelet in the end of the post by bending it around a pair of round-nose pliers (see Basic techniques, page 17).

2 Cut the chain into the following lengths: one 40 cm (15¾ in) long, one 10 cm (4 in), two 8.5 cm (3⁵⁄₁₆ in), two 7 cm (2¾ in), two 5.5 cm (2⅜ in), two 4 cm (1½ in), two 2.5 cm (1 in), and two 5 mm (two links). Lay the various lengths of chain out on your work surface in the order that they will be used on the necklace. The longest (40 cm/15¾ in) piece of chain is the

necklace itself. The 10 cm (4 in) length is for the central pendant and the remaining pairs of shorter lengths should graduate in size on either side of the central pendant.

3 Attach the chain lengths to the necklace by opening the top link of each chain and attaching it to a link in the necklace chain (see the instructions for opening jump rings in Basic techniques, page 16). Begin with the 10 cm (4 in) chain, linking it in the middle of the 40 cm (15¾ in) length. Continue to attach the remaining pendants to the central necklace with one empty link separating each chain from its neighbour (see the photograph).

three Attach the chains to the necklace with one empty link between each one.

step four Attach three beads to the bottom of each pendant chain.

4 Open the eyelets of the 11 mm ($^7/_{16}$ in) and 16 mm ($^5/_8$ in) purple bead assemblies using snipe-nose pliers, and link them to the end of all 13 chain drops, using the three largest beads on the three longest pendant chains in the middle of the necklace. Attach the round beads to either side of the chain link above the purple oval bead drops. Repeat on all 13 chains. There will be one beaded head pin left over.

5 Link seven jump rings together. Attach them to one end of the necklace chain and finish by linking the remaining bead to the last ring. Link the clasp to the other end of the necklace chain, using the last jump ring.

Hint

To make a simple pair of matching earrings, use two 4 cm (1$^5/_8$ in) lengths of chain, add the same trio of beads as on the pendant chains and attach earring hooks at the other end of the chain.

Clip-on earrings

Form follows function in clip-on earrings:

because the clasp is necessarily quite large

to hold the weight of the earring on the ear in

relative comfort, clip-on earrings are often quite

extravagant in size and composition. This design

incorporates a glittering cluster of faceted

crystals and round glass beads in smoky hues.

Materials
Earring frame: 17 mm (⅝ in) silver domes and
   clip-on backs
32 silver head pins, 15 mm (⅝ in) long
8 round crystal beads, 6 mm (¼ in) diameter
12 bicone crystal beads, 6 mm (¼ in) diameter
12 round beads, 6 mm (¼ in) diameter

Tools
Round-nose pliers
Snipe-nose pliers
Flat-nose pliers
Side cutters
Safety glasses

step one Thread individual beads onto head pins.

step three Secure the beads by looping the ends of the posts at the back of the

Hints

This design may also be used to make shoe clips. Clip the earring on to a strappy shoe or remove the clip with end cutters and glue onto the shoe for a more permanent solution.

Make more of a statement by adding feathers to the cluster of beads. Glue a feather to the earring back before securing the dome. Make sure the feather is glued in the correct position so it sits appropriately when worn.

1 Thread individual beads onto head pins and divide them into two equal groups containing the same number of beads of each shape and colour. Do not cut or bend the posts at this stage.

2 Begin to position the beads on the silver dome, working from left to right. Thread a beaded head pin through the perforated dome so the bead sits against the convex side. Cut the post with the side cutters, leaving approximately 7 mm (¼ in) of pin protruding at the back.

3 As you go, turn the dome over and loop the post of the head pin you have just

four Repeat steps two and three until all beads are used.

step five Crimp the metal tabs to secure the earring back.

inserted (see Basic techniques, page 17) using the round-nose pliers. (See the photograph above for details.) Make sure the pin holds the bead securely to the frame. You may want to secure it in place with the snipe-nose pliers. Make sure the loops at the back of the dome aren't too big, or it will be difficult to secure to the earring back.

4 Attach the remaining beads by repeating steps two and three until all the beads are used. Randomly position the different shaped and coloured beads across the dome, noting the arrangement so that you can repeat it for the second earring.

5 When both domes are completely beaded and secure, attach the earring backs. Fit the back to the dome. If you have difficulty positioning the components closely together, clamp the edges of both pieces with the flat- or snipe-nose pliers. Secure the pieces by pushing the metal tabs flat over the edge of the dome one at a time, with the snipe-nose pliers.

Beaded flower

This charming three-dimensional decoration

is simple to construct, and suits many purposes:

it could be worn in the hair or as a brooch, used

to decorate a gift, or attached to a hat.

Materials
204 bicone crystals, 5 mm (3/16 in) diameter
Silver artist's wire
Green florist's tape

Tools
Snipe-nose pliers
Side cutters
Safety glasses
Scissors

step two Thread crystals onto the middle of each length of wire.

step three Create a petal and twist the ends of the wire to secure it.

1 Cut the artist's wire, using the side cutters, into three 12 cm (4¾ in) lengths, four 15 cm (6 in) lengths and five 17 cm (6¾ in) lengths.

2 Thread crystals onto the middle of each length of wire: 10 crystals each on the 12 cm (4¾ in) lengths, 16 crystals each on the 15 cm (6 in) lengths and 22 crystals each on the 17 cm (6¾ in) lengths.

3 Loop the wire together and twist approximately 20 mm (¾ in) of the excess wire together to secure the beads as a petal. Gently bend the crystal petal so it sits at a slight angle to the wire stem.

4 Construct the flower from the inside out. Cut a 40 cm (15¾ in) piece of wire and bend 4 cm (1½ in) of the wire at a right angle. Hold the three smallest crystal loops in a bunch, and place the bent end of the wire on the stems. Wrap the long piece of wire around the stems three times, as shown in the photograph above.

5 Next, position the medium-sized crystal loops around the first three and secure as for Step 4, using the tail of the same long piece of wire.

6 Position the large crystal loops around the outside of the flower and secure in the

four Construct the flower from the inside out.

step five Secure the stems together with the tail of the wire.

same manner, twisting the wire tightly so the whole form is secured. Cut the excess wire away using the side cutters.

7 For a short stem, cut the remaining wires leaving 20–30 mm (¾–1¼ in). Twist the wires together so there are no sharp edges and cover completely with green florist's tape. Wrap the tape around the wires like a bandage, making sure all of the wire is covered and any sharp ends are tucked in. Adjust the angle of the petals until you have a flower shape that you are pleased with.

Hints

Use this technique to make a decoration for a brooch or a hair comb. Complete the flower as above to Step 4. Cut the wire stems, leaving 20–30 mm (¾–1¼ in). Separate half of the stems in one direction and half in the opposite and press the wire out flat. Secure the flower to a brooch pin or comb using florist's green tape: simply wrap the tape around the wire and the brooch or comb frame.

Evening bag

A simple satin clutch purse is an evening-wear essential. Add some sparkle in the form of a satin bow encrusted with crystal flower beads.

The beads are stitched to wire-edged satin ribbon and, although it may seem like a fiddly task at first, there could be nothing quicker and easier than this stitching project once you get into the rhythm of beading.

Materials
Ribbon: wide ribbon with a tight satin weave and wire edges (these will support the beads)
Flat flower crystals with a hole through the middle
Seed beads
Clutch purse (the example shown is satin)

Tools
Needle and cotton thread (to match the colour of your ribbon)
Fabric glue (PVA), or glue to suit the material from which your bag is made; for example, leather will require a specialty glue
Scissors
Clear nail varnish

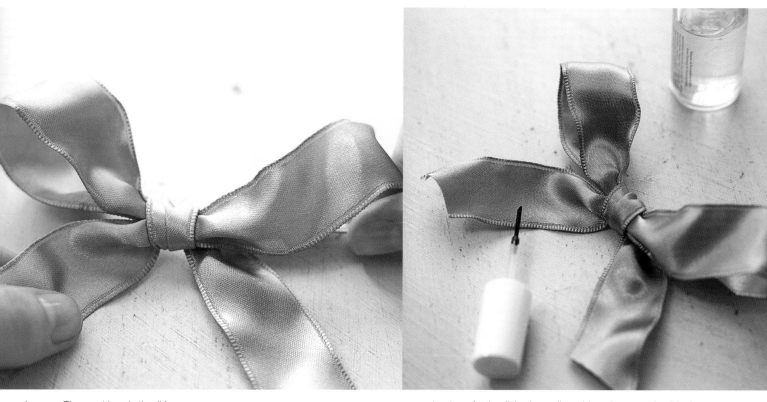

step one Tie a neat bow in the ribbon.

step two Apply a little clear nail varnish to the cut ends of the bow.

Hints

Decorate a tote bag by sewing flat embellished ribbon around the top and bottom of the bag.

You could also use this technique to attach the beaded ribbon to a cushion.

In this example the seed beads are the same colour as the flower crystals, but you could create a different effect by using contrasting colours.

1 Tie a neat bow with the ribbon, making sure it sits flat and is not too tight. The wire edges will help to hold the bow in an appealing shape. Test out the bow on the bag to determine the size of the bow — in our example, it is about half the length and two-thirds of the height of the bag.

2 Trim the ends of the ribbon and apply a little clear nail varnish to the cut edge, to prevent fraying.

3 Cut a 150 cm (60 in) length of sewing cotton, thread into the needle and knot the ends together so that you have a doubled thread 75 cm (30 in) long.

four Sew flower crystals onto the ribbon, using seed beads to anchor the thread.

step six Apply glue to the back of the ribbon.

4 Start to bead the ribbon. Pass the thread through the ribbon and thread a flower crystal and a seed bead onto the needle. Push the beads along the thread until they sit on top of the ribbon. Thread the needle back through the flower crystal and the ribbon. Pull the thread firmly to secure the beads in place. Repeat this process, making sure the thread is pulled firmly through each bead.

5 When beading the bow's loops, pass the needle and thread through only the top layer, which will create a three-dimensional look. (If you'd like the bow to be flat, sew through both layers).

6 When the beading is complete, push the bow into the desired shape. Apply glue to the back of the ribbon at strategic points such as towards the outer ends of the loops (not too close to the ends, or the bow will be pulled flat against the bag) and behind the knot. Position the bow on the front flap of the bag and allow the glue to dry completely before using the bag.

Drop cluster earrings

These little grapelike clusters frame the face and provide movement and sparkle. Silver findings and opaque white beads as in the pictured example result in a simple, delicate look. Smoky crystals and blackened findings would give a more sultry effect, or combine beads in a variety of colours and finishes for a bolder approach.

Materials

34 head pins, 4 mm (3/16 in) long

16 jump rings, 4 mm (3/16 in) diameter

1 pair earring hooks

34 opaque white oval beads, 7 x 6 mm
  (1/4 x 5/16 in) diameter

Tools

Side cutters

Safety glasses

Round-nose pliers

Snipe-nose pliers

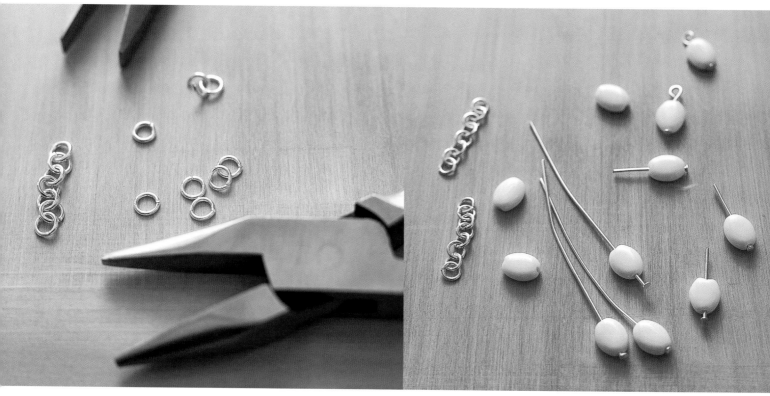

step one Using the snipe-nose pliers, connect the jump rings into two lengths of eight.

step two Thread each bead onto a head pin and cut the posts to the correct leng

1 Connect the jump rings together into two lengths of eight using the snipe-nose pliers (see Basic techniques, page 16).

2 Thread each bead onto a head pin and trim the excess wire with end cutters. Trim 32 of the pins to leave 7 mm (⁵⁄₁₆ in) excess and 2 pins to leave 15 mm (⁵⁄₈ in) excess.

3 Attach the earring hook to the jump rings with the snipe-nose pliers.

4 Connect the beaded head pins to the jump rings using the snipe-nose pliers (see Basic techniques, page 19). Swing open and attach the longest head pin to the last free jump ring, and then connect a shorter beaded pin either side. Continue attaching the remaining beaded pins either side of the jump rings until you reach the top.

5 Repeat this process to make a pair.

three Attach the earring hook to the top of the jump rings.

step four Connect the beaded head pins to the jump rings.

Variations

By altering the size of the components used, you can create multiple styles using the same technique. To either reduce or extend the length of the earrings, simply add or deduct jump rings, but always hang three beads off the last jump ring to complete the earring.

If you use larger beads, also use larger jump rings so that the proportions of the earring remain the same and the beads have enough room to hang elegantly.

You can also use this technique to make a matching bracelet or necklace. Use a belcher chain instead of jump rings and make all of the beaded end posts the same length. Fasten with a parrot clasp.

Beaded tablecloth

A square of delicate tulle is edged with a garland of seed beads to make a table cover. Use it on its own or over the top of a fabric cloth as shown in the photograph at left.

Materials
104 cm (41 in) square of tulle
100 g (3½ oz) silver seed beads

Tools
Needle and sewing thread
Scissors
Ruler

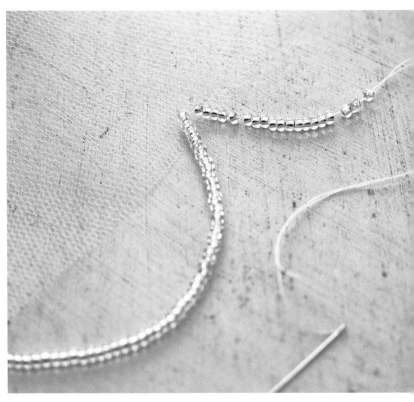

steps three and four Secure the loops at 8 cm (3⅛ in) intervals.

1 Cut the tulle to size, ensuring that it is perfectly square.

2 Thread 100 cm (40 in) of sewing thread on the needle, so the cotton is doubled and the final length is 50 cm (20 in). This will be enough thread to make five or six beaded loops. Secure the cotton to a corner of the tablecloth and thread on 10 cm (4 in) of seed beads.

3 Measure 8 cm (3⅛ in) along the tulle edge from the corner where you started and secure the cotton thread. Pass the needle though the tulle from the front to back, across three holes, then pass it through to the front. Draw through all of the remaining thread so that the loop of beads hangs in a gentle curve.

4 Thread another 10 cm (4 in) of seed beads onto the needle and secure the end of this loop at a further 8 cm (3⅛ in) interval. Repeat this process until the bead loops hang all the way around the tulle. Each side of the tablecloth should hold 13 sections of beads.

Hints

Attach beaded tassels (see pages 50–53) to the corners of this tablecloth for more glamour.

Change the proportions of the design by altering the length and width of the tulle to suit your table. Work in multiples of 8 cm (3⅛ in) to ensure that the loops of beads are shown to best effect.

Create a pretty, layered effect by making a couple of cloths in different sizes and laying one on top of the other.

Brooch

In this design, a large kilt pin supports multiple strands of chain dressed with beads, charms and other trinkets.

This is a rather heavy item, so is best worn with thick or heavy-weight winter garments. Use it to decorate a jacket or coat lapel, or to fasten a woollen shawl over your shoulders.

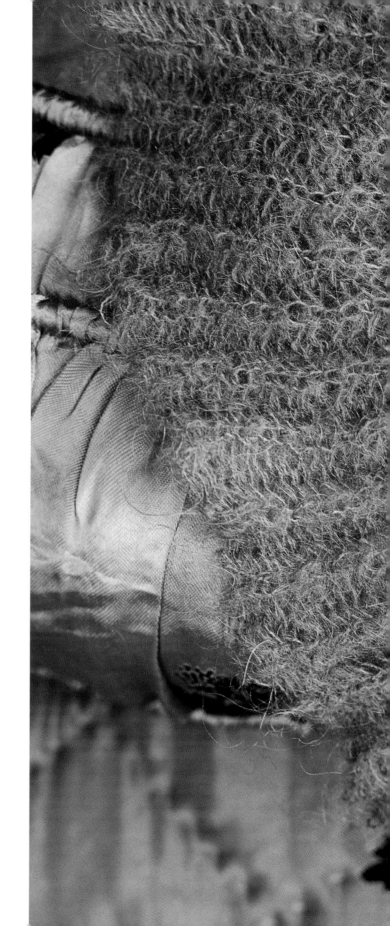

Materials

Large safety pin (kilt pin)

Blackened chain, 25 cm (10 in) each of
  five types

Artist's wire, 0.6 mm (22 gauge)

11 blackened head pins, 40 mm (1½ in) long

6 blackened eye pins

Assorted grey, purple and blackened silver
  beads (approximately 23 beads in total)

Tools

Round-nose pliers

Snipe-nose pliers

Side cutters

Safety glasses

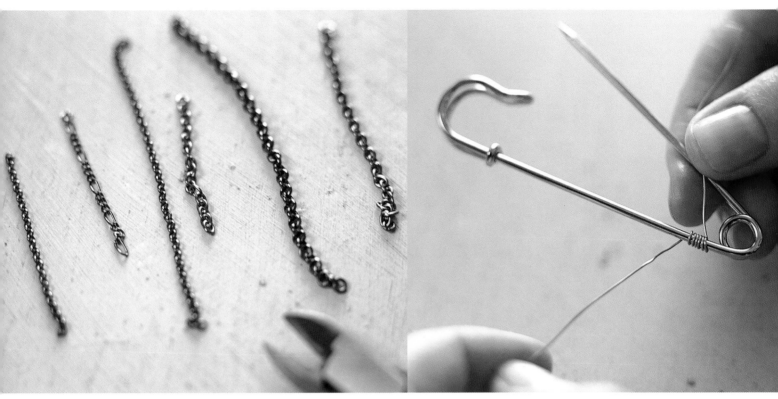

step one Cut the chains into random lengths.

step two Attach the artist's wire to the bar of the kilt pin.

1 Cut the various pieces of chain into 19 random lengths of 11–20 cm (4¼–8 in), using side cutters.

2 Connect one end of each length of chain to the brooch pin using the artist's wire. First, cut a piece of wire approximately 1 m (40 in) long. Bend the last 5 cm (2 in) of the wire at a right angle; this piece will act as a handle while the rest of the wire is wrapped around the pin. Undo the pin (this makes it easier to wrap the wire) and wrap the wire diagonally around the enclosed side of the pin five times, beginning at the right-angle bend. Push the coiled wire tightly together to make it compact.

3 Thread a piece of chain onto the wire and wrap the wire another three times around the bar of the pin, to allow room for the chain to hang loose from the pin. Add another piece of chain and wrap the wire around the bar of the pin another three times. Repeat this process until all 19 pieces of chain are attached.

4 Once all of the chains are connected to the bar of the pin, wrap the remaining wire five times around it and cut the wire. If the chain and wire do not run the entire length of the bar of the pin, wrap the remaining wire at either end of the bar so the chains are tight and centred.

o three Wire the lengths of chain to the brooch bar.

step seven Add beaded head pins to selected lengths of chain.

5 Thread 14 beads onto 12 head pins (two of the pins will have two beads) and cut the end of each pin with side cutters, leaving 10 mm (⅜ in) of post. Using round-nose pliers, create an eyelet (see Basic techniques, page 17). Using the remaining beads, thread one to three beads onto each eye pin, then cut posts and create an eyelet.

6 Attach the six beaded eye pin sections to the brooch by integrating them into the lengths of chain. Select the heights and positions for the eye pins then cut the chain at the appropriate point using side cutters. Link the eye pins onto the chain using snipe-nose pliers.

7 Lastly, randomly attach the 12 beaded end posts onto the base of any of the 15 lengths of chain. Make sure the beads are positioned at different lengths and look balanced across the brooch.

Christmas decorations

Welcome the festive season by adorning

rooms and the branches of evergreen trees

with sparkling decorations in jewel colours.

These bright decorations could be modified

and used as gift-wrapping decorations and

even festive earrings, if you wish.

Materials (for each decoration)
Memory wire in large bangle shape
31 silver head pins, 20 mm (¾ in) long
2 silver eye pins, 20 mm (¾ in) long
20 cm of small belcher chain with 3 mm
   (⅛ in) links
82 silver seed beads, 3 mm (⅛ in) diameter
46 white plastic pearls, 4 mm (³⁄₁₆ in) diameter
1 Swarovski crystal drop with side holes,
   18 mm (1¹⁄₁₆ in) long

Tools
Round-nose pliers
Snipe-nose pliers
Safety glasses

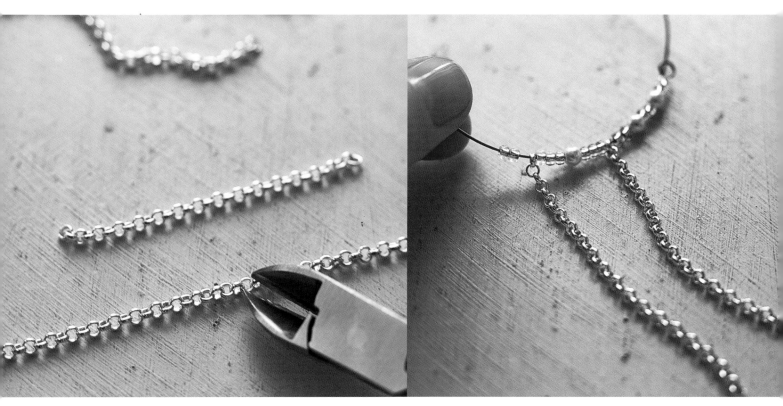

step two Cut the belcher chain to length using side cutters.

step four Begin threading beads, pearls and chain onto the memory wire.

1 Cut the memory wire into a 22 cm (8¾ in) length using side cutters and create a loop at one end using the round-nose pliers (see Basic techniques, page 17).

2 Use the side cutters to cut the belcher chain into one 55 mm (2³⁄₁₆ in) length (29 chain links) and one 68 mm (2¾ in) length (35 chain links).

3 Thread beads onto the head pins: thread 15 pins with two seed beads on each and 16 pins with a single pearl on each. Cut the head pins with side cutters, leaving 10 mm (³⁄₈ in), and then create a loop (see Basic techniques, page 17).

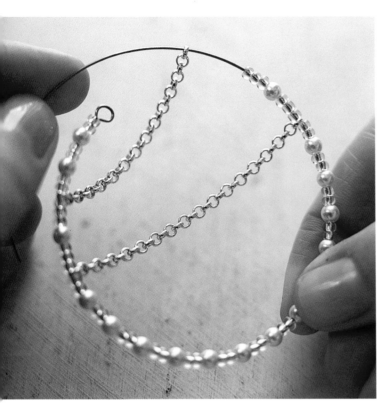

4 Thread the beads and chain onto the memory wire in the following sequence: two seed beads, one pearl, two seed beads, one pearl, two seed beads, one end of a 55 mm (2³⁄₁₆ in) length of belcher chain, three seed beads, one pearl, three seed beads, one end of a 68 mm (2¹¹⁄₁₆ in) chain. Next thread on two seed beads and one pearl and repeat this process 13 times.

5 Now thread on two seed beads, then the loose end of the 68 mm (2¹¹⁄₁₆ in) length of belcher chain (making sure the chain is not twisted). Repeat the same combination of beads and chain as on the opposite side of the decoration, but in reverse order to make sure the beading is symmetrical: three seed beads, one pearl, three seed beads, the loose end of the 55 mm (2³⁄₁₆ in) length of belcher chain (making sure the chain is not twisted), two seed beads, one pearl, two seed beads, one pearl and two seed beads.

6 To complete the circular form and make sure the beads sit tightly together, cut off the excess memory wire leaving 10 mm (³⁄₈ in) and loop the cut end into an eyelet using the round-nose pliers.

step seven Attach the beaded head pins to the chains.

7 Attach the beaded head pins to the chain. Use seven pearl and seven seed bead drops for the top chain and nine pearl and eight seed bead drops for the bottom chain.

8 Attach the first post to the first loose chain link, making sure the bead is hanging straight. Repeat this process using every second link of chain, alternating pearls and seed beads (see the photographs above and on page 85 for details).

9 Cut 32 mm (1¼ in) of belcher chain (15 links) and attach either end of this length of chain to each rounded end of the memory wire using snipe-nose pliers (see

Basic techniques, page 19). Using the same technique, attach an eye pin to the middle link of the chain. Bend the post of the eye pin around the base of the round-nose pliers to create a large hook (by which you will hang the decoration).

10 Lastly, thread the 18 mm (¾ in) Swarovski crystal drop onto an eye pin and create a loop at the post end, making sure this loop is flat and sitting in the same plane as the eye. Open the loops with snipe-nose pliers and hook them into the loops on either end of the memory wire (underneath the chain). This final connection will hold the circular shape in place.

p eight Alternate beads and pearls across the chain links.

step ten Attach the Swarovski crystal droplet.

Variations

Use this design to make earrings by following the steps above and adding an earring hook to the top of the chain instead of an eye pin. You may like to use small bangle memory wire for smaller hoops, adjusting the lengths of chain and numbers of beads as appropriate.

For alternative Christmas decorations, link frilly crystal drops and two-holed crystals together with jump rings, as used in the Chandelier (pages 30–33), and hang them with earring hooks or loops of wire.

Belt

The buckle of this belt is made from a brooch
frame (available from craft and haberdashery
suppliers) encrusted with pearl and crystal
beads and attached to a length of ribbon.
Velvet, satin and grosgrain (petersham) ribbons
are all suitable.

A smaller brooch frame and narrower ribbon could
be used to transform the design into a choker.

Materials

1 m (39 in) ribbon, 2.5 cm (1 in) wide
Cotton thread in a colour to match the ribbon
1 round brooch frame, 3.5 cm (1⅜ in) diameter
66 head pins, 50–60 mm (2–2⅜ in) long
33 crystal beads, 6 mm (¼ inch) diameter
33 pearl beads, 6 mm (¼ inch) diameter

Tools

Round-nose pliers
Snipe-nose pliers
Side cutters
Safety glasses
Needle
Scissors
Clear nail varnish

step one Thread beads onto head pins.

step two Bend head pin posts around the round-nose pliers.

1 Thread each individual bead onto a head pin (see the photograph above).

2 Bend the posts of the head pins around the base of the round-nose pliers to create a large, loose loop (see Basic techniques, page 17, and the photograph above).

3 Position the beaded head pins on the brooch frame and wrap the posts around the frame using round-nose pliers and snipe-nose pliers (see Basic techniques, page 18). Repeat this process until all of the beads are secured onto the frame. Cut off the excess posts using side cutters.

4 Measure the desired length of ribbon and cut the ends at right angles. Coat each cut end with a small amount of clear nail polish to stop the ribbon from fraying.

5 When the nail varnish is dry, thread the ribbon around the central bar of the brooch frame and fold the end back on itself. Stitch the double ribbon together using small slip stitches, to secure the ribbon to the frame. Feed the loose end of the ribbon through the frame to cinch the belt.

step three Twist the head pin posts around the brooch frame.

step five Stitch the ribbon around the frame's central bar to secure it.

Variations

Use this design to dress up an old evening bag. Pass a length of ribbon through the frame and stitch the ribbon to the bag. Alternatively, make a handle of ribbon attached to the bag at one end and passed through a D-ring at the other end. Slide the buckle along the ribbon to shorten or lengthen the handle as desired.

You could also use the brooch frame and ribbon as a curtain tie or as a pull cord for a window blind.

Shoe jewellery

Ideal for a wedding, a formal ball or any other
special occasion, shoe jewellery is simple to
make but adds a designer touch to plain footwear.

Materials

50 cm (30 in) chain

80 head pins, 30 mm (1¼ in) long

80 bell caps, 5 mm (³⁄₁₆ in) diameter

22 pearls, 10 mm (³⁄₁₆ in) diameter

36 pearls, 7 mm (¼ in) diameter

12 round AB crystals, 6 mm (¼ in) diameter

10 round diamante beads

Tools

Round-nose pliers

Snipe-nose pliers

Side cutters

Safety glasses

Craft glue, suitable for leather and metal

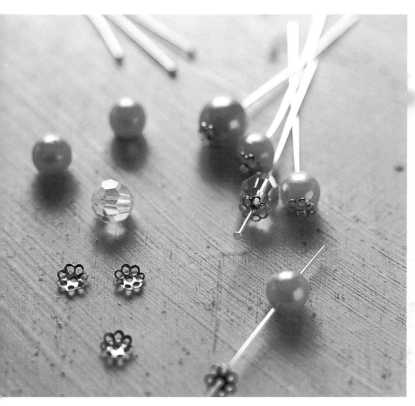

step one Thread a bell cap and a bead onto each head pin.

step four Add beads to the lengths of chain.

Hints

If you do not want to glue the chain to your shoes, take the shoes and the chain (without the beads attached) to a boot maker and have the chain sewn onto the shoes in the appropriate position at intervals. Once the chain is in place, attach all of the beads.

You may want to use plastic beads and pearls instead of glass as they weigh much less.

1 Thread a bell cap, curved side up, and a bead onto each head pin. Using side cutters, trim off the head pin post leaving 10 mm (⅜ in). Make a loop in the end of the post by wrapping it around the round-nose pliers (see Basic techniques, page 17).

2 Cut the chain into two 11 cm (4⅜ in) lengths and two 13 cm (5⅛ in) lengths, using the side cutters.

3 Sort the beads into four similar groups — one group for each chain length. Two of the groups should have a few more beads in them than the others, but all should have the same balance of colour and shape.

‌p five Glue the middle of the longer piece of chain to the shoe.

step six Glue the shorter piece of chain above the first.

Divide each group in half again, with one half of the beads to be applied to the chain before it is attached and the other half to be added after the chain is attached.

4 Using the snipe-nose pliers, open the loops on the beaded head pins and attach half of the beads to the lengths of chain, ensuring that the assortment is varied but similar on each chain. Make sure all the beads hang in the same direction.

5 Glue the 13 cm (5⅛ in) length of chain to the shoe first. Run a short, thin line of glue (if the glue is too thick it will block the chain links) approximately 15 mm (⅝ in) below the front of the shoe. When the glue is tacky, position the chain across the front of the shoe. When the glue is dry, repeat the process with both sides of the chain. Gluing the middle section first will make it easier to position the rest of the chain.

6 Repeat the process, gluing the 11 cm (4⅜ in) length of chain above the first, approximately 5 mm (³⁄₁₆ in) from the front of the shoe.

7 When both of the chains are secured and the glue has dried, attach the remaining beads randomly to the chain links across the front of the shoe.

Cuff

This exuberantly embellished cuff bracelet
features rows of sparkling seed beads and
a cluster of pearls and gems in its centre.

Materials

Memory wire in small bangle shape
4 separator bars, 7-hole (approximately
   3.5 cm or 1⅜ in long)
12 cm (4⅝ in) belcher chain, medium size;
   alternatively, you can link sixty 4 mm (³⁄₁₆ in)
   jump rings
28 silver head pins, 30 mm (1¼ in) long
2 cream pearls, 15 mm (⅝ in) diameter
8 cream pearls, 12 mm (½ in) diameter
6 cream pearls, 7 mm (¼ in) diameter
2 Czech crystals, clear AB 11 mm
   (⁷⁄₁₆ in) diameter
2 Czech crystals, clear AB 10 mm
   (⅜ in) diameter
7 pink AB beads, 7 mm (¼ in) diameter
364 pink seed beads, 4 mm (³⁄₁₆ in) diameter

Tools

Side cutters
Safety glasses
Round-nose pliers
Snipe-nose pliers

step one Thread beads onto head pins then make loops in the ends of the posts.

step four Construct the first row of the cuff.

1 Thread beads (except for the seed beads) onto head pins. Cut the posts with side cutters, leaving 10 mm (⅜ in) of post, and create an eyelet using the round-nose pliers (see Basic techniques, page 17). Divide the beads into three similar groups.

2 Cut the belcher chain into three 85 mm (3⅜ in) lengths or link three lengths of 18 x 4 mm (³⁄₁₆ in) jump rings.

3 Cut the memory wire with side cutters into seven 22 cm (5 in) lengths. Create a loop in one end of each length by bending the wire around the round-nose pliers (see Basic techniques, page 17).

4 Begin constructing the seven rows of the cuff. For row one, thread the memory wire through a spacer bar, then thread on the components in the following order: 20 seed beads, a second spacer bar, 12 seed beads, a third spacer bar, 20 seed beads, and a fourth spacer bar. Finish the row by making a loop in the end of the wire close to the bar, so that the beads sit tightly together.

5 Repeat this process for rows 3, 5 and 7.

6 For row two, thread a spacer bar then the other components in the following order: 20 seed beads, a second spacer bar, one seed bead then one length of chain

step six Add the lengths of belcher chain to the even numbered rows.

step eight Attach the groups of beads to the chains.

(through the first link). Continue to thread 10 seed beads, and then thread on the last link of chain, so the links sit across the top of the seed beads. Continue threading components in this order: one seed bead, the third spacer bar, 20 seed beads, and the fourth spacer bar. Finish by making a loop in the end of the memory wire (as above).

7 Repeat this process for rows 4 and 6.

8 Link the beaded head pins (see Basic techniques, page 19) onto the chains one at a time, using the smaller beads on the outsides and a large one in the middle. Repeat this process for each section of chain.

Hints

Belcher chain is preferable for this design to jump rings, which may open over time.

To turn this design into a choker, use 38 cm (15 in) of necklace memory wire and add two extra spacer bar sections around each side for support.

Lantern
candle holder

The luminous glow of flickering candle light is increased and refracted by rows of seed beads in these glittering lanterns. Don't be daunted by the number of beads used in the construction: the method is quite simple and surprisingly quick to complete.

Materials

For the small lantern: 864 round Indian glass
   beads, 4 mm (³⁄₁₆ in) diameter
For the large lantern: 1560 round Indian glass
   beads, 4 mm (³⁄₁₆ in) diameter
Artist's wire, gold 0.7 mm (21 gauge)

Tools

Round-nose pliers
Side cutters
Safety glasses
Ruler

step two Create a noose at the end of the wire, then thread all of the beads on.

step four Add the spokes of doubled wire.

1 Cut the artist's wire with the side cutters into six 70 cm (20 in) lengths. Bend each length in half and set them aside.

2 Unwind the remaining artist's wire, keeping it coiled. Create a wrapped loop in the end of the wire (see Basic techniques, page 18) with the round-nose and snipe-nose pliers. Cut off the excess wire so that only a round loop is left at the end of the wire.

3 Thread all of the beads onto the coiled wire, carefully moving them along to the end of the wire, while still keeping it coiled.

4 Thread the wires made in Step 1 onto the beaded coil, placing the first wire through the looped end of the beaded coil. Continue to thread wires 2 to 5 along the beaded coil, placing a bead in between each wire (see photograph). Secure the long wires around the coil by pulling them open in opposite directions.

5 Form the base of the lantern by continuing to wrap the beads around the initial loop, forming a flat disc. Secure each rotation of the beads with the long wires by passing them around either side of the coil. Expand the base by adding

p five Construct the flat base of the lantern.

step six Create the vertical sides of the lantern.

an extra bead in between the wires on each roation (see photograph) until there are eight beads in between each wire. Push the beads tightly together after completing each coil so that the lantern is even.

6 Construct the vertical walls of the lantern by continuing to coil and secure the beads, maintaining eight beads in each section. The first row of the wall should rest on top of the last row of the base. Continue to secure the coils until all the beads are used.

7 Once all beads are secured, twist the remaining lengths of doubled wire for approximately 20 mm (¾ in), cut off any excess with side cutters and bend the wires so they sit inside the lantern. Push the lantern into a cylindrical shape.

Beaded curtain

Here, the hem of a plain curtain is decorated with loops of glass seed beads to catch the sunlight. You could use the same technique of wire loops to decorate a pendant lampshade, or to create a wall-hanging from a fabric panel. Match the design by stitching beads in the same scalloped pattern onto a cushion cover to coordinate your soft furnishings in a room.

Materials
Memory wire in large bangle shape
100 g (3½ oz) seed beads
Netting or sheer curtain to fit the length and
    width of the window, hemmed and finished
    for hanging as you prefer
Tassel; ready-made (from haberdashery store)
    or handmade (see page 50)
Ribbon, 5 mm (³⁄₁₆ in) x twice the length of
    the curtain

Tools
Round-nose pliers
Flat-nose pliers
Needle and sewing thread
Metal snips for cutting steel; these are the best
    tool to cut the memory wire as they have
    stronger blades than end or side cutters
Fabric glue

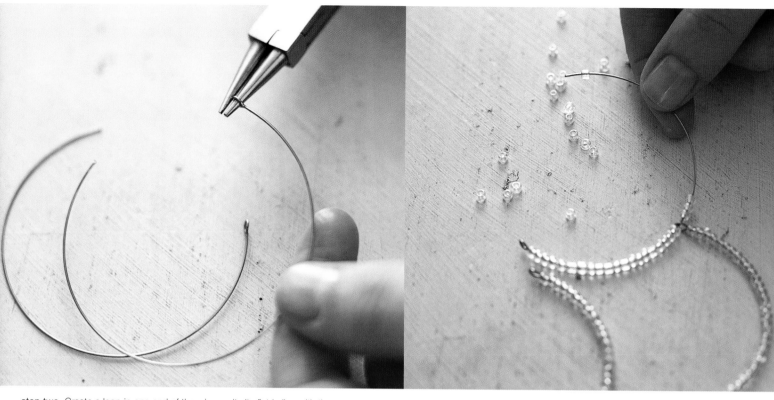

step two Create a loop in one end of the wire, so it sits flat in line with the curve.

step five Thread the loops of the previous row onto the memory wire with the bea▮

1 Cut the memory wire with the metal snips into 15 cm (6 in) lengths. The memory wire will hold its 'U' shape.

2 Loop one end of the memory wire with the end of the round-nose pliers, creating a 3–4 mm (⅛ in) loop. Create the loop so it sits at a right angle but in line with the curve of the memory wire.

3 Construct the curtain in rows, working from the bottom tip of the triangle upwards. Use one 'U' shaped wire for the first row and an additional 'U' shape for every new row, up to row 11 or the desired width of the curtain.

4 Row 1: take a looped 'U' shaped memory wire and thread on 43 seed beads. Loop the end of the memory wire to hold the beads tight and to match the other side.

5 Row 2: Thread 23 seed beads onto a 'U' shape. Thread the wire through the left-hand side loop of row one. Thread another 20 seed beads on and create a loop in the end as before. Take another 'U' shape and thread 20 seed beads on, thread through the right-hand side loop of row 1, add 23 beads and create an end loop.

6 Row 3: Thread 23 seed beads onto a 'U' shape. Thread through the left-hand side

step six Add three seed beads between the loops of the memory wire.

step seven Sew the loops of the final row to the hem of the curtain.

loop of the first 'U' shape of row two. Thread another 20 seed beads on and create a loop in the end as before. Take another 'U' shape and thread 20 seed beads on, then thread through the right-hand side loop of the 'U' shape of row two. Thread on three seed beads and the loop of the left-hand side of the next 'U' below. Thread on 20 seed beads and loop the end. Repeat this process for every 'U' shape in the row, completing the last 'U' shape with 23 seed beads as before.

7 When you have constructed 11 rows (or the appropriate number for your curtain), sew the top row to the base of the curtain.

8 Glue ribbon along the side of the net curtain. When the glue is dry you may hang the curtain and complete it by adding the tassel. A purchased tassel from a haberdashery store may be used, as in the photographs, or use a beaded tassel such as the one on pages 50–53.

Hints

Choose a range of seed beads in graduated colours and use a different colour on each row.

Instead of using three beads in between each 'U' shape you could substitute a teardrop-shaped bead.

This design would work well on a frosted bathroom window or a similar window where the curtain does not need to be lifted up and down for privacy or to show a view.

Index

Published in 2006 by Murdoch Books Pty Limited
www.murdochbooks.com.au

Murdoch Books Australia
Pier 8/9, 23 Hickson Road, Millers Point NSW 2000
Phone: +61 (0) 2 8220 2000   Fax: +61 (0) 2 8220 2558

Murdoch Books UK Limited
Erico House, 6th Floor North, 93–99 Upper Richmond Road, Putney, London SW15 2TG
Phone: +44 (0) 20 8785 5995   Fax: +44 (0) 20 8785 5985

Chief Executive: Juliet Rogers
Publisher: Kay Scarlett

Design concept: Tracy Loughlin
Art direction: Vivien Valk
Designer: Jacqueline Richards
Project manager: Janine Flew
Editor: Melody Lord
Photographer: Natasha Milne
Stylist: Sarah O'Brien
Production: Monika Paratore
Project designer and maker: Elizabeth Bower (elizabethbower.com.au)

National Library of Australia Cataloguing-in-Publication Data
Bower, Elizabeth.
Bead. Includes index.
ISBN 9 78174045 7446. ISBN 1 74045 744 7.
1. Beadwork. 2. Beads. I. Title. (Series : Handmade style). 745.582

Printed by 1010 Printing International Limited in 2006. PRINTED IN CHINA.

Vegetables

Text by John Fenton-Smith
Photographs by Lorna Rose

WHITECAP
BOOKS